Kate Gregson

CAMBRIDGE

Our Book

6 Our Furniture
page 47

8 In the Kitchen
page 63

5 Our Activities
page 39

7 At Home
page 55

9 In the Wild
page 71

Sounds   page 79

Numbers   page 88

3

Our Friends

 Look.  Circle.  Say.

1 Weather

 Listen.  Look. Circle.

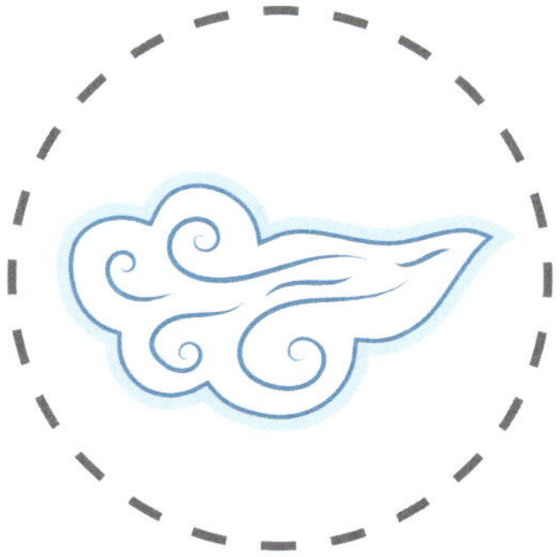

windy

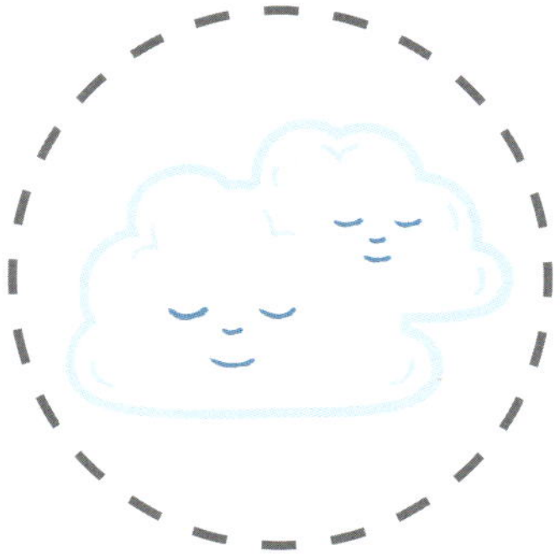

cloudy

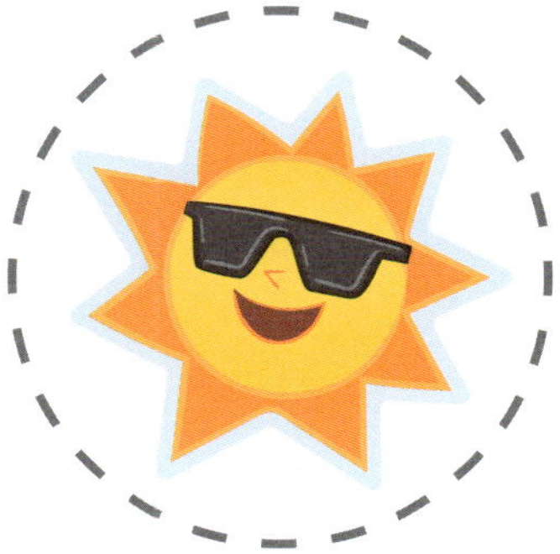

sunny

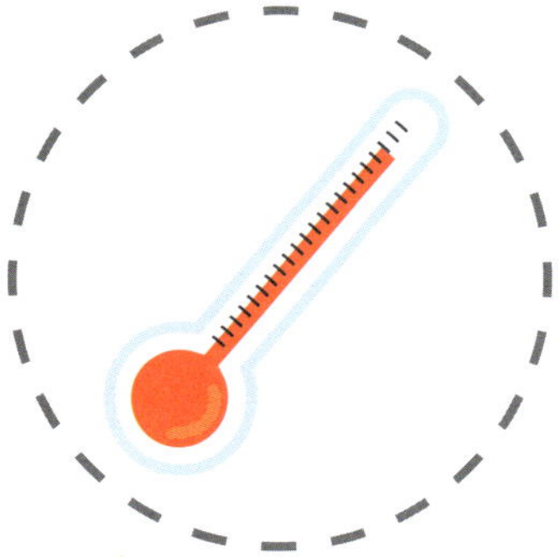

hot

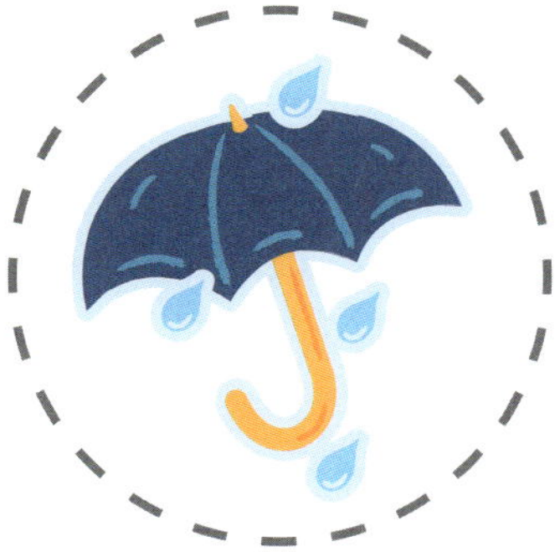

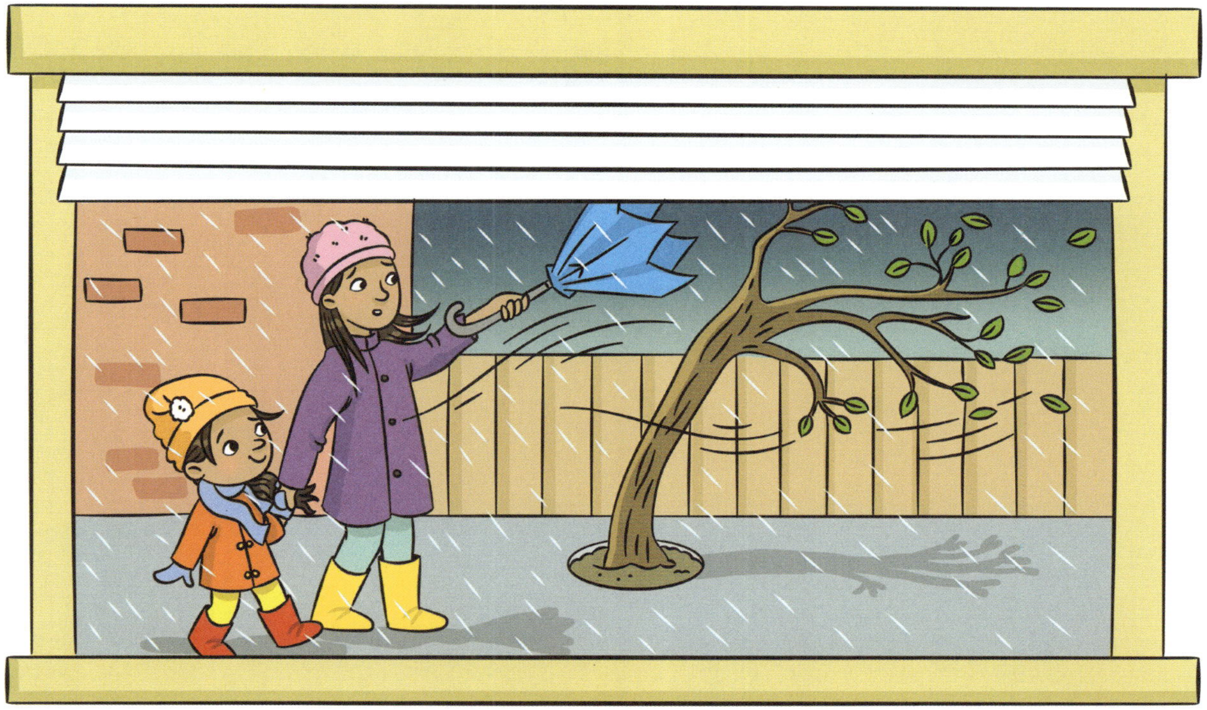

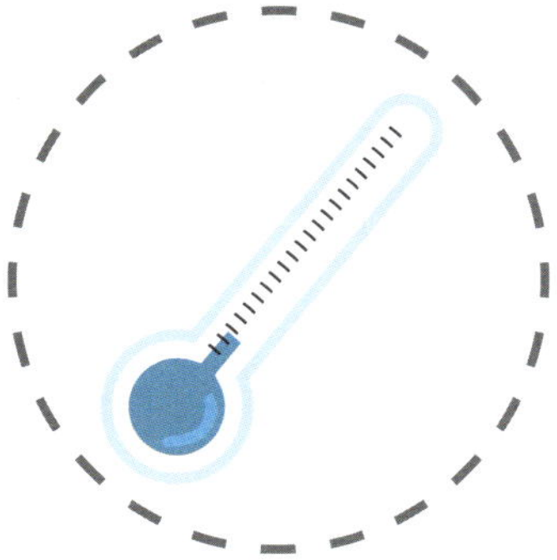

cold

rainy

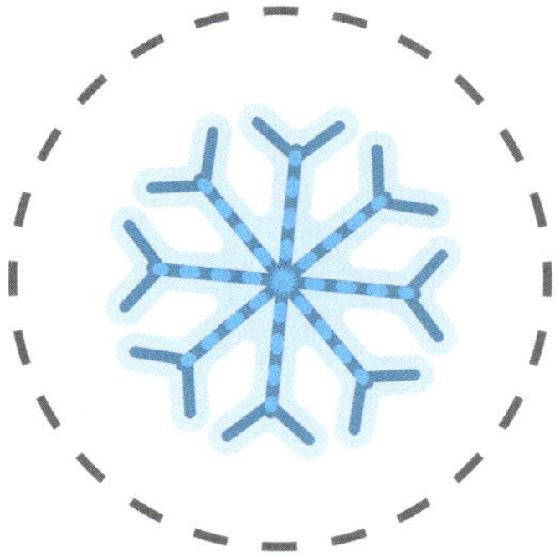

snowy

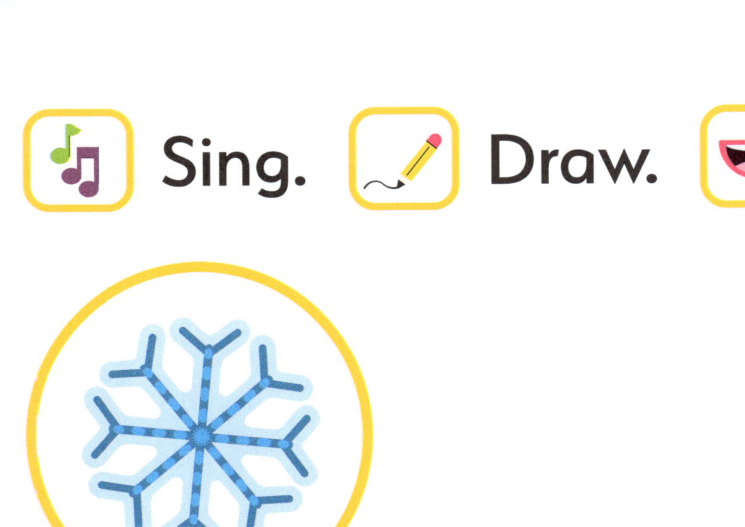

🎵 Sing. ✏️ Draw. 👄 Say.

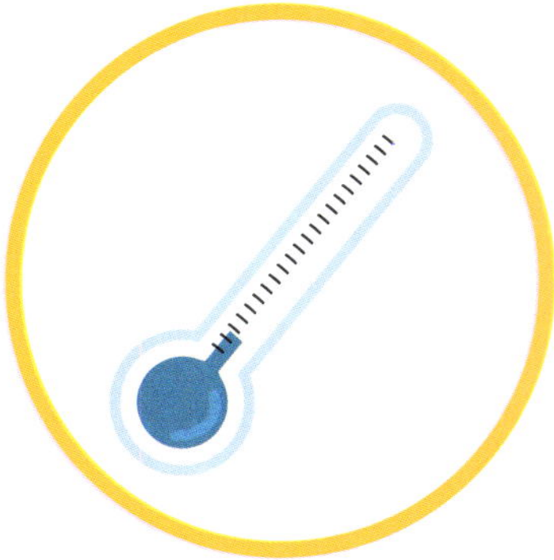

 Think.  Look.  Circle.

 Look.  Think.  Circle.

 Look.  Think.  Match.

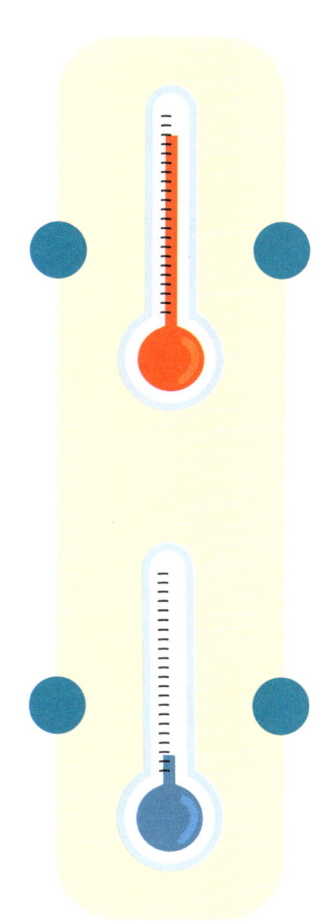

  # Make. Say.

 Look.  Think.  Color.

   Unit 1   **Well-being:** I feel like I'm safe.

2 Our Families

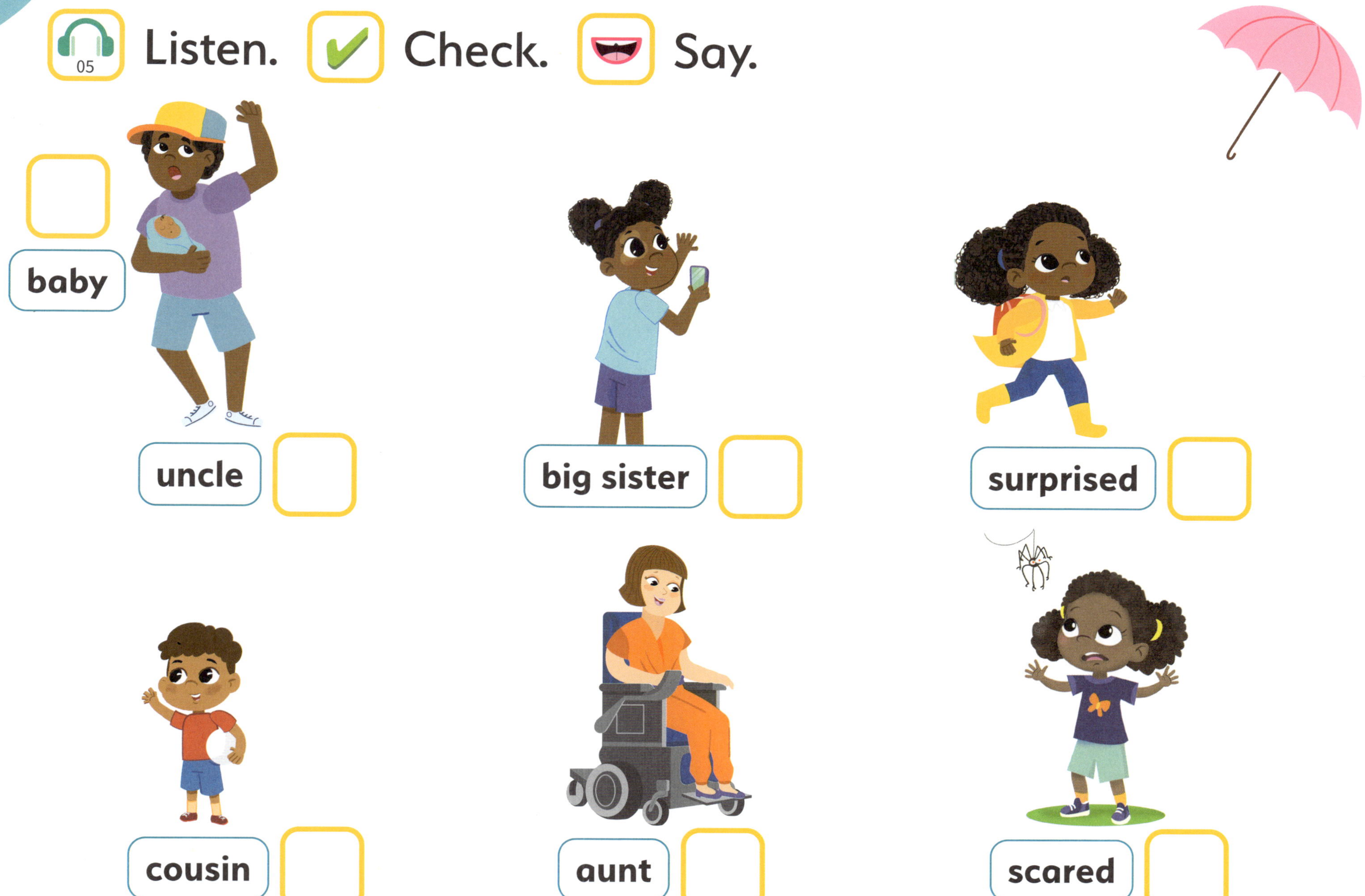

 Listen.  Draw.  Say.

 Look.  Say.  Match.

 Make.  Say.

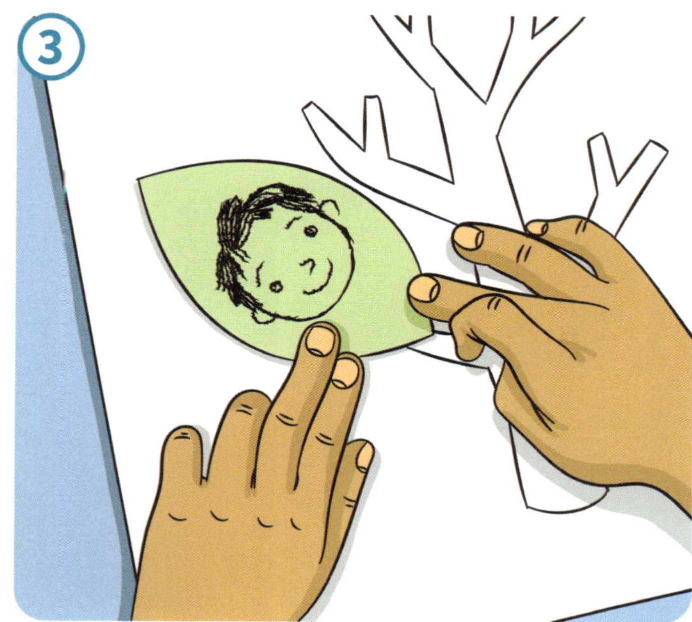

3 Our Places

 Listen.  Point.  Color.

park

library

pool

store

playground

beach

market

 Point.  Color.  Say.

 **Listen.**  **Follow.**  **Say.**

 Look.  Match.

 Look.  Think.  Color.

 Unit 3 **Cross-curricular:** social studies

 Make.  Say.

 Say.  Draw.

4 Our Colors and Shapes

 Match.  Color.  Listen.

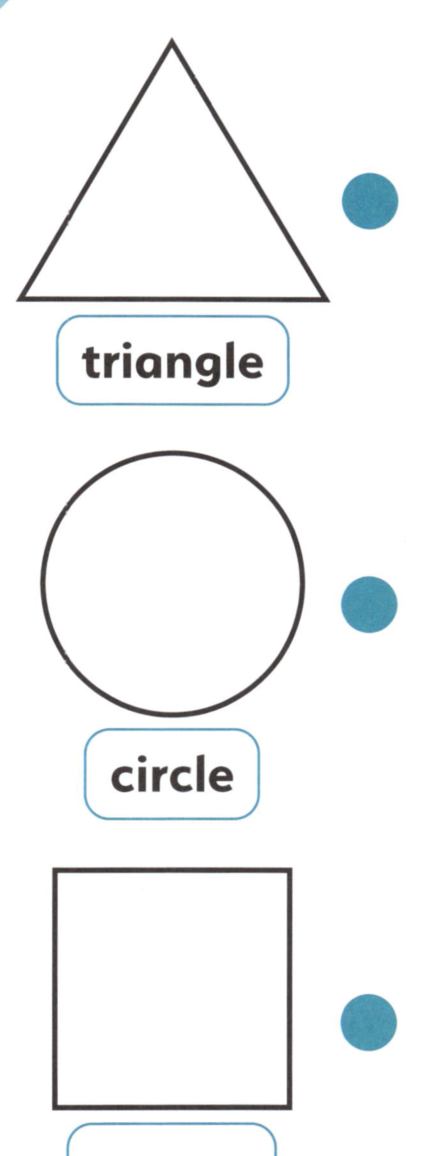

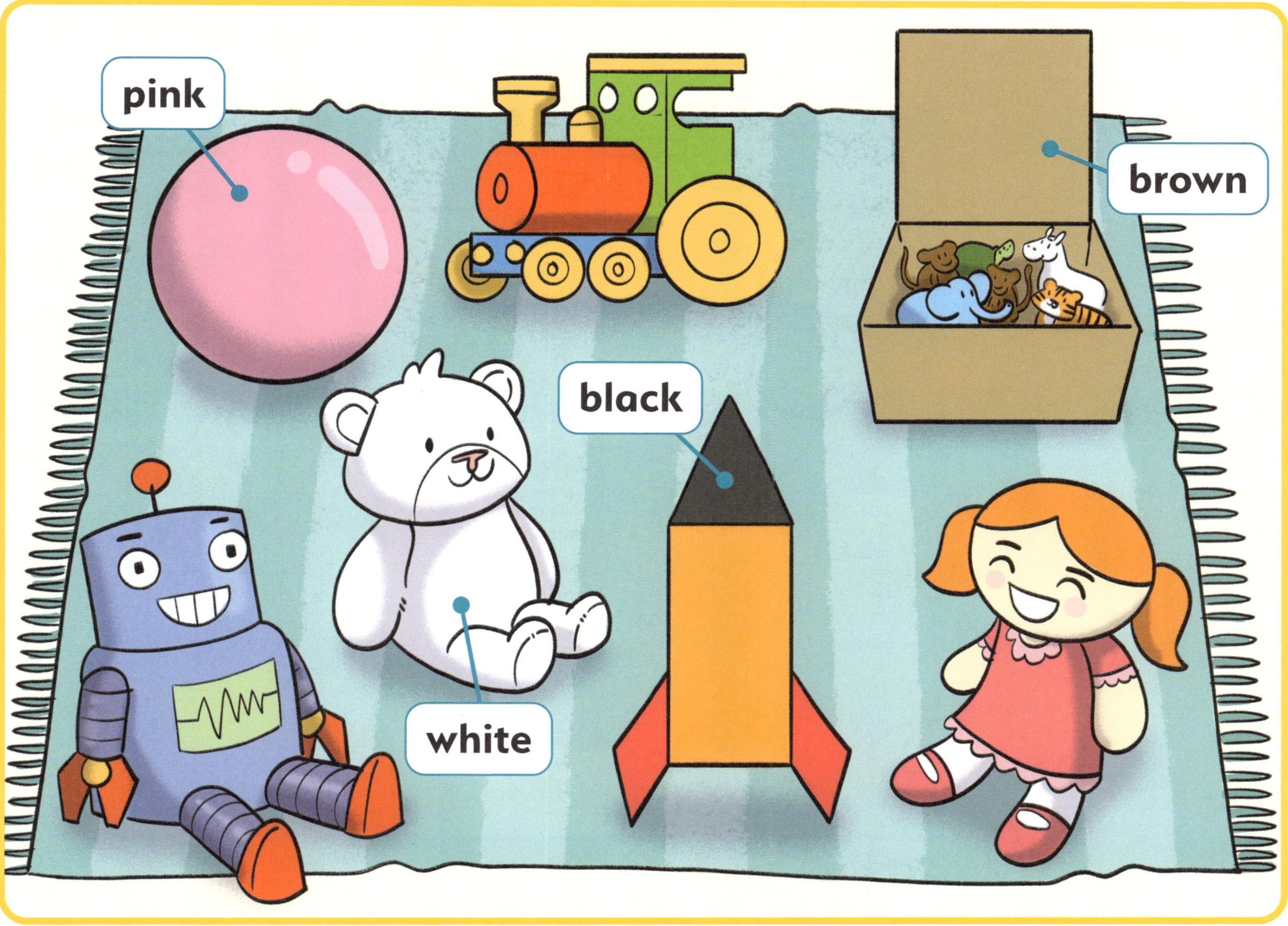

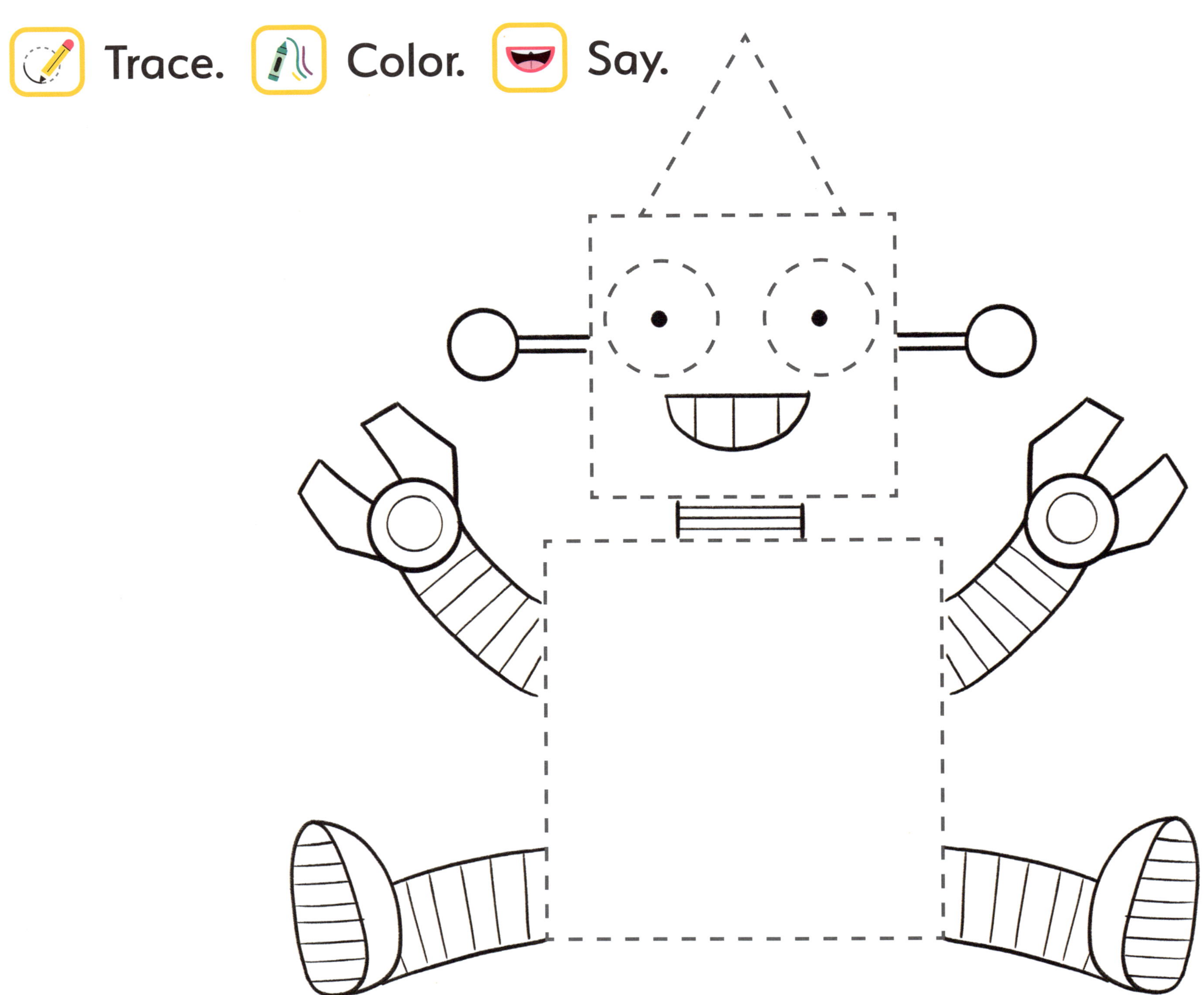

10 Listen. Draw. Color.

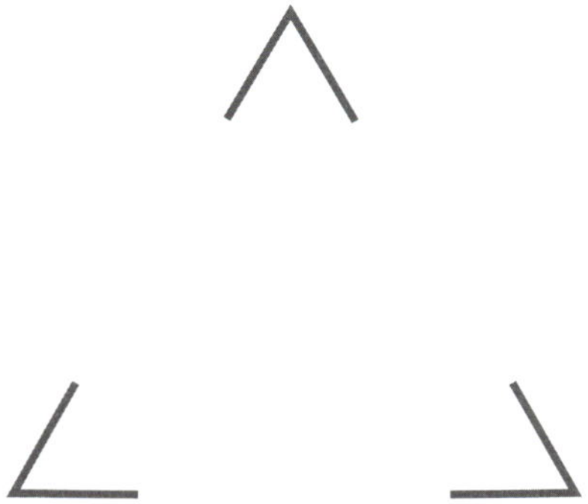

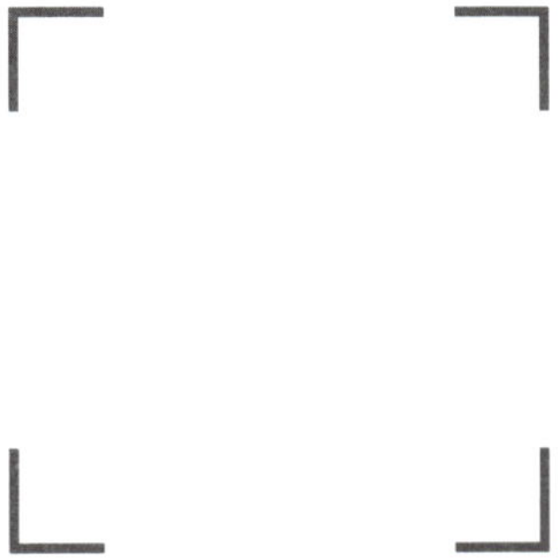

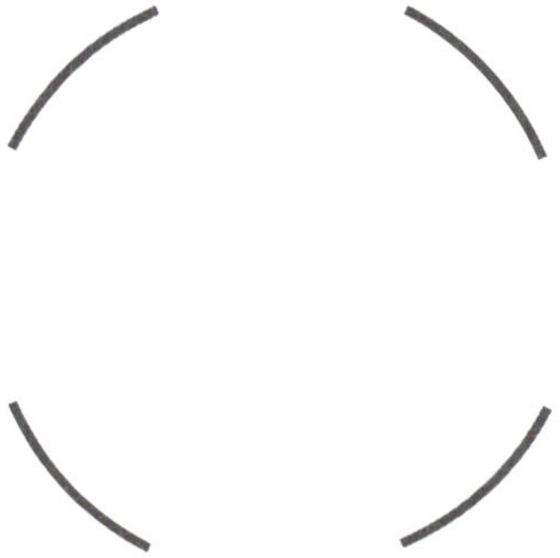

Language Presentation: Draw a (circle). Color the (circle pink). What color is it?

 Think.  Look.  Match.

1

2

3

 **Count.**  **Think.**  **Trace.**

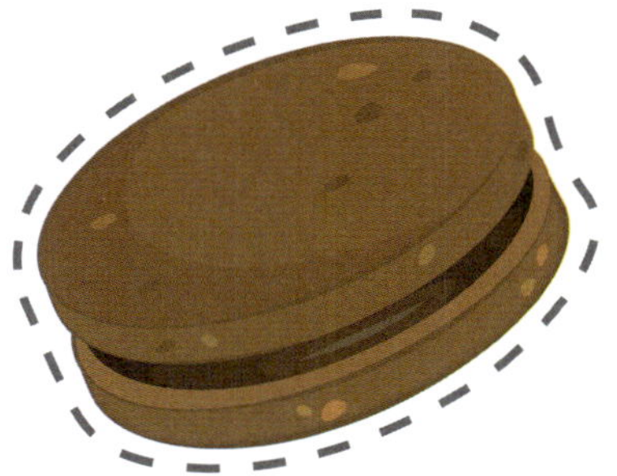

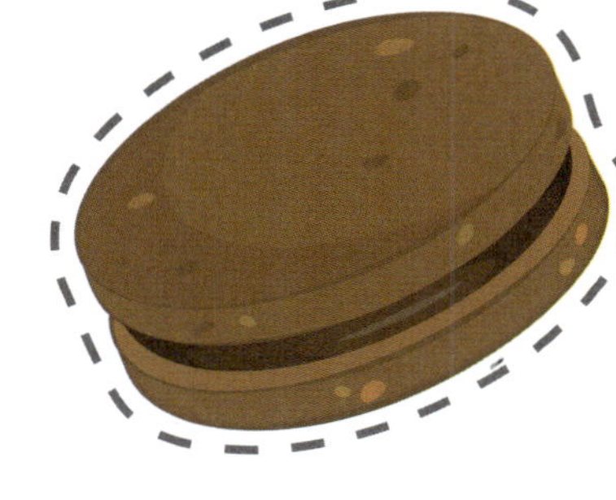

 Look.  Color.

 Make.  Say.

Our Activities

 Listen.  Say.  Match.

jump

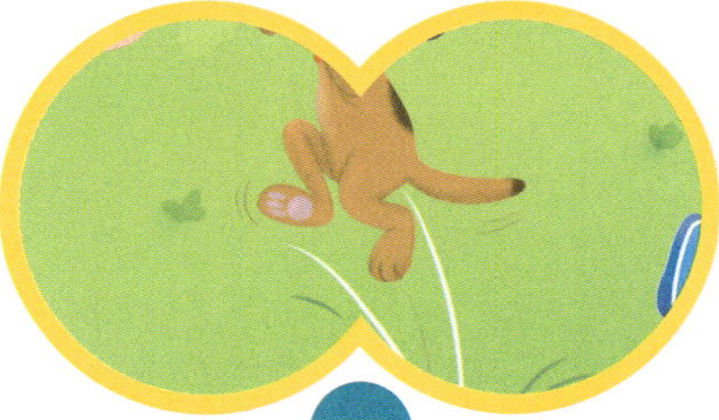

throw

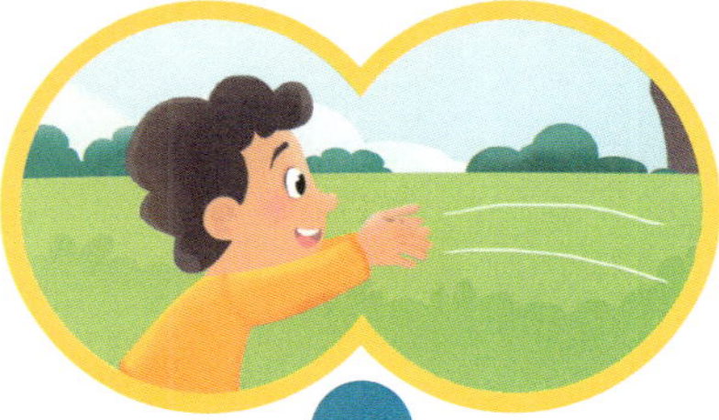

catch

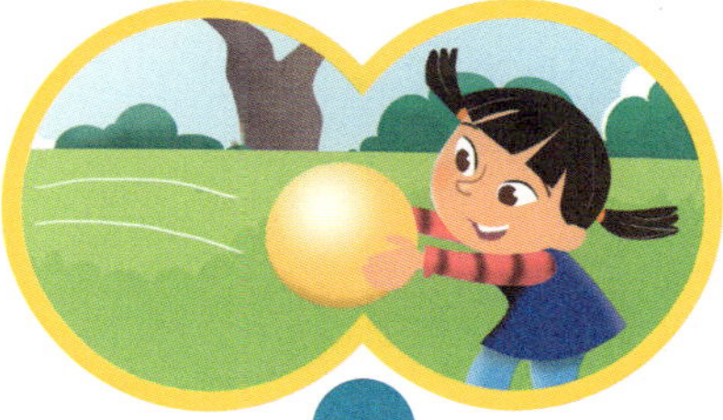

sing

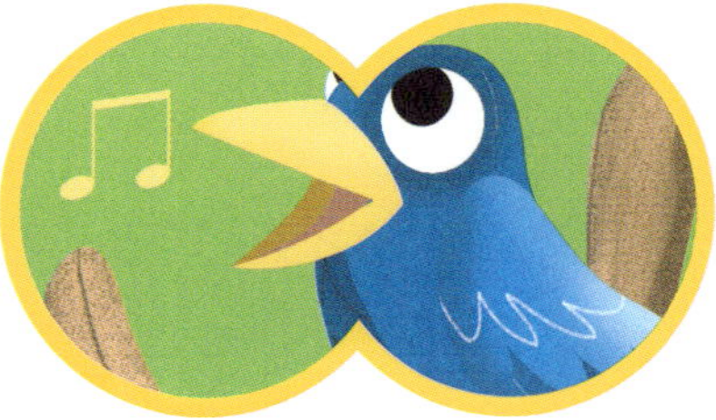

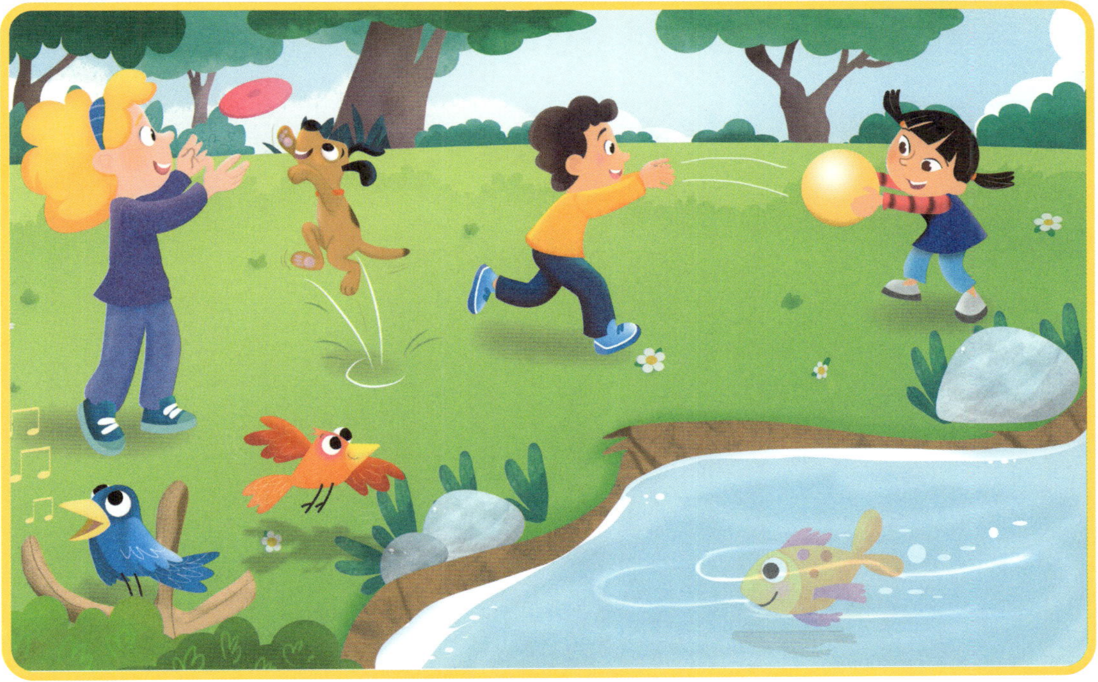

swim

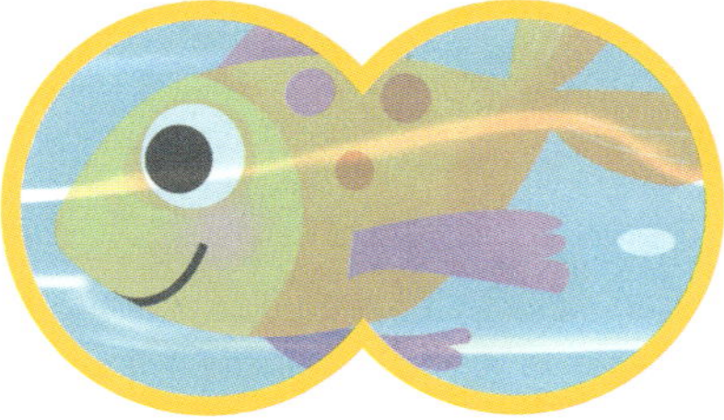

fly

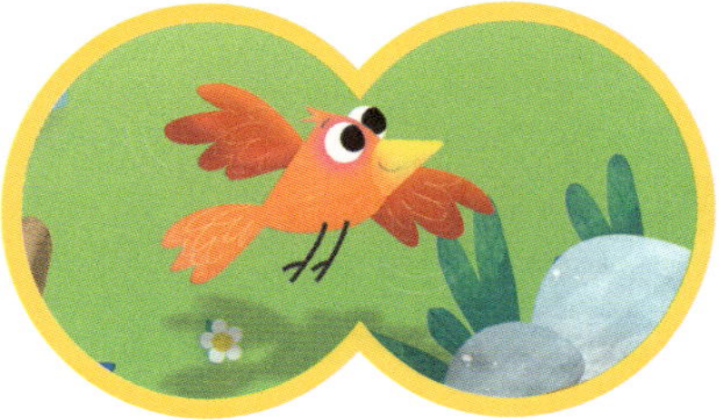

run

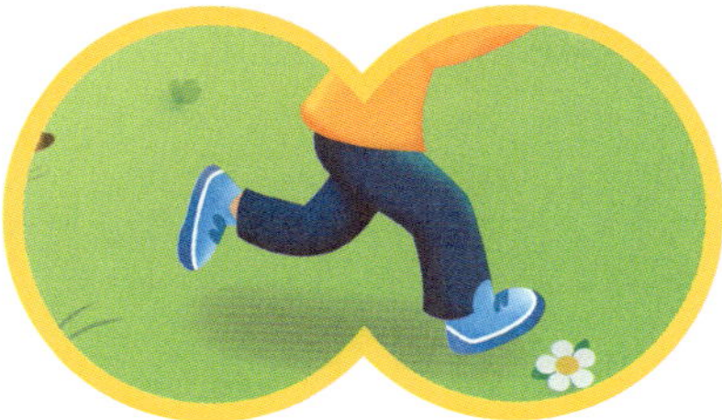

 Look.  Color.  Draw.

6 Our Furniture

  Find.  Match.  Draw.

shelf

chair

table

toy box

bed

floor

couch

 Color.  Think.  Draw.

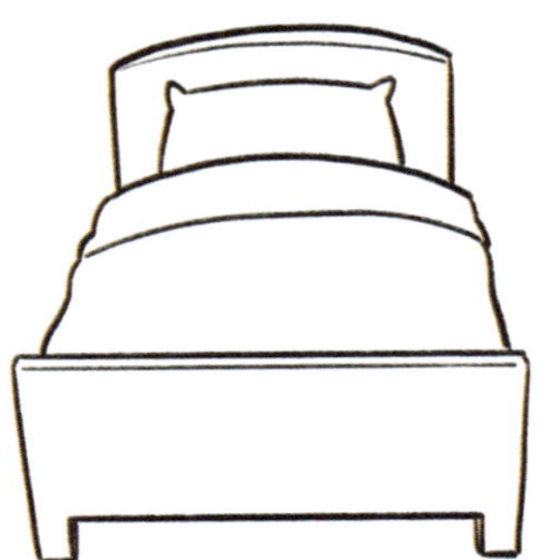    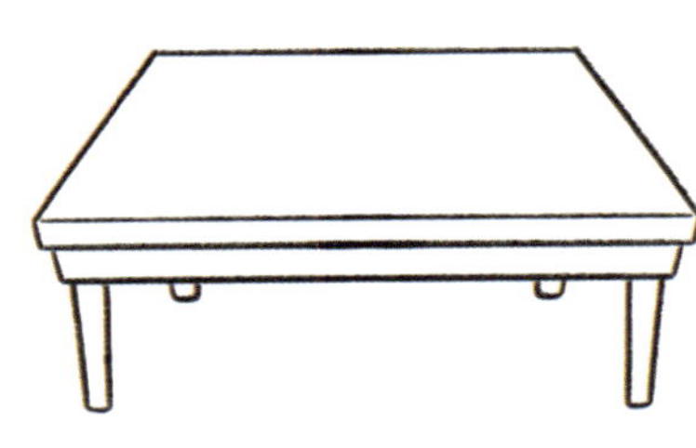

 Unit 6 Vocabulary Practice

 Look.  Circle.  Draw.

 Look.  Think.  Match.

 Unit 6 **Cross-curricular:** science

 Make.  Say.

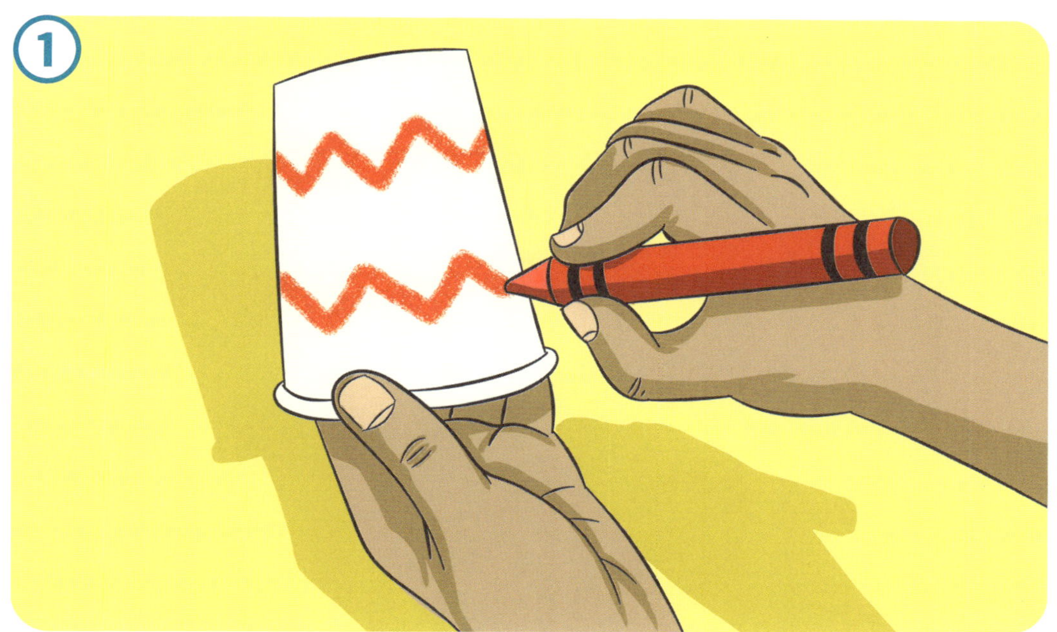

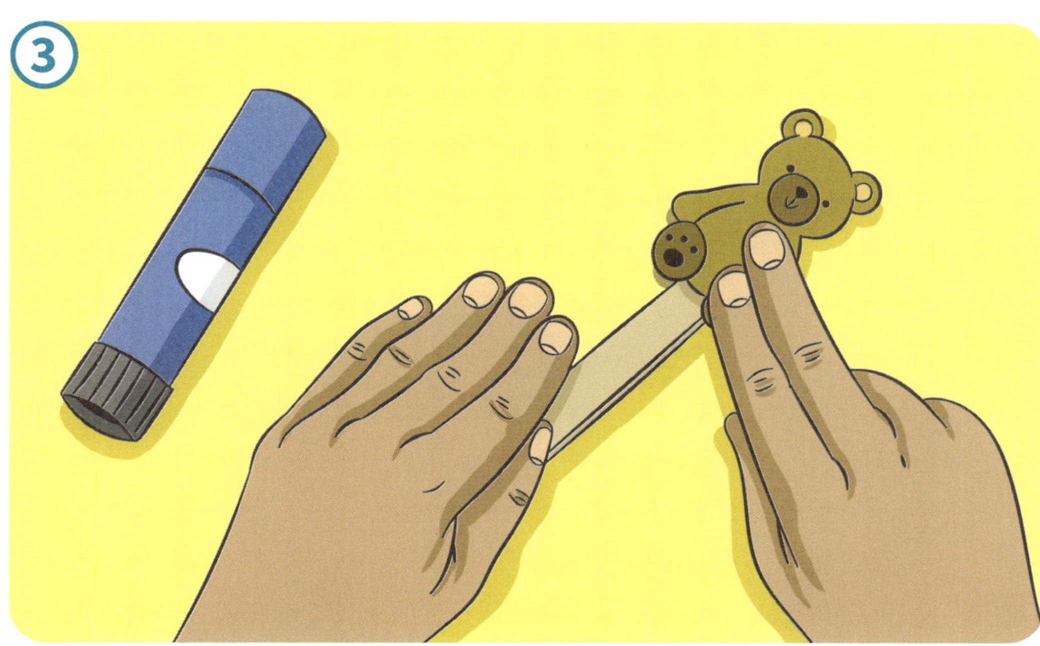

 Think.  Check.  Draw.

 Well-being: I feel like a lot of things are exciting.

7 At Home

 Listen.  Follow.  Color.

new

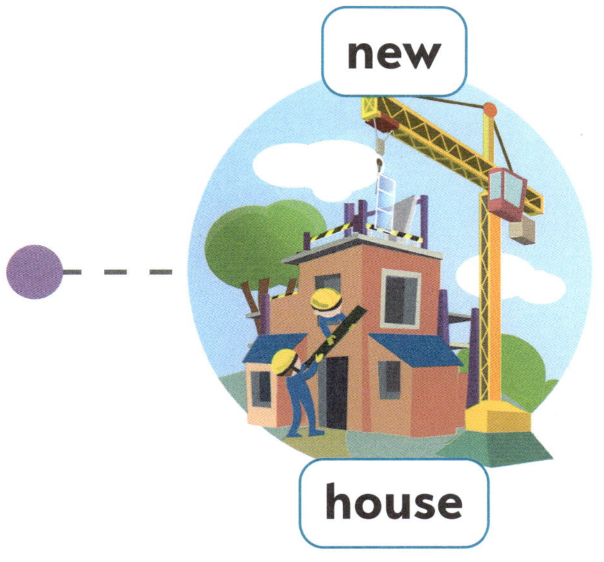

house

old

tree

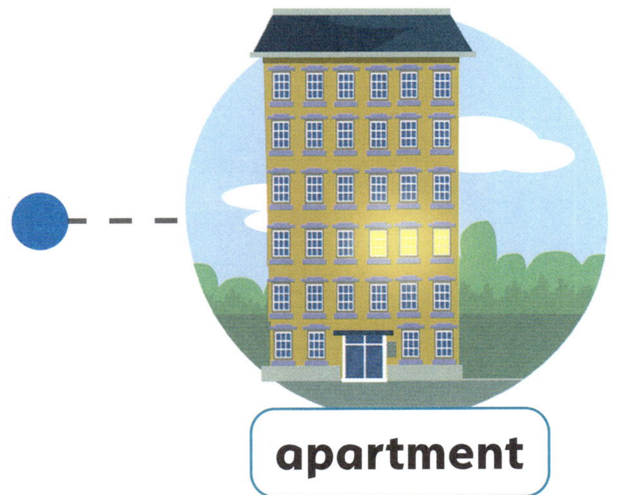

apartment

pond

yard

 Think.  Draw.  Say.

Think. Draw.

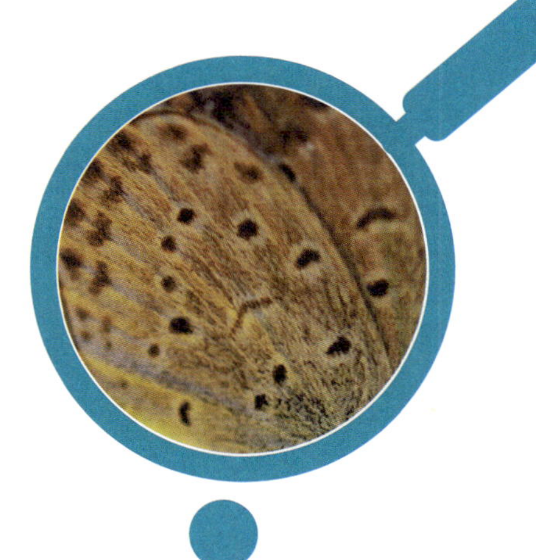
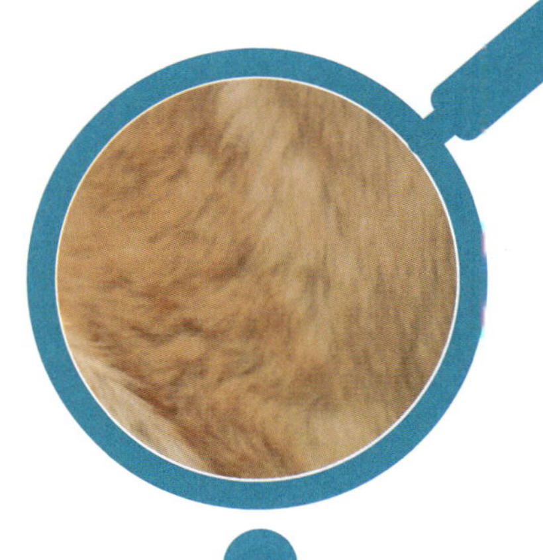
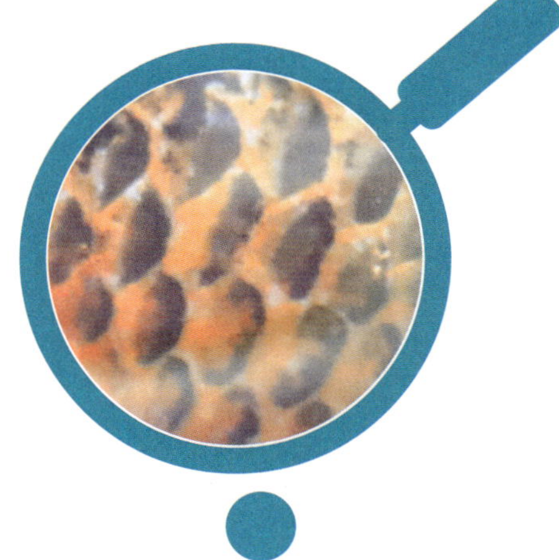

Make. Say.

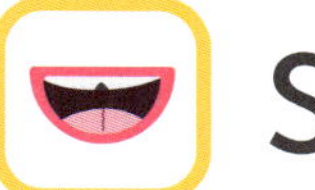

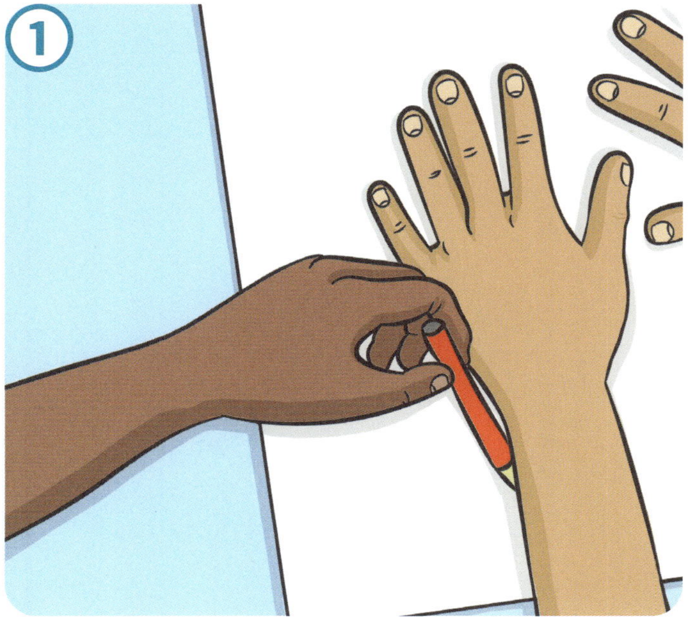

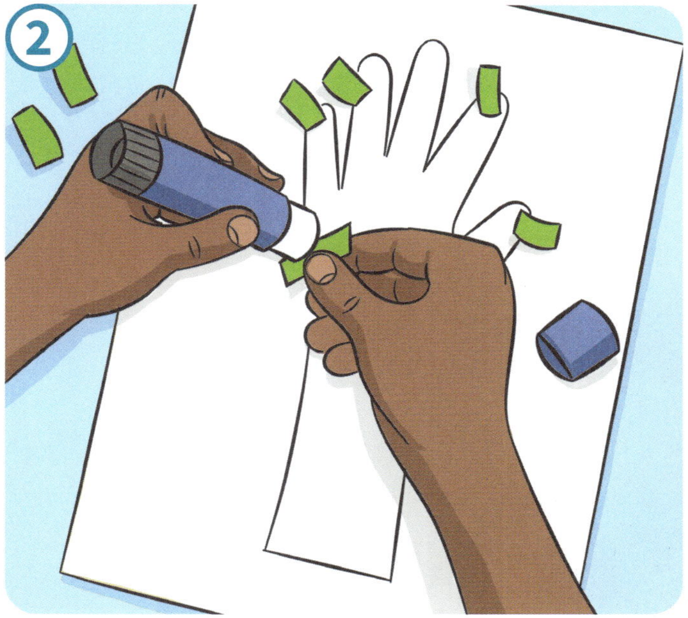

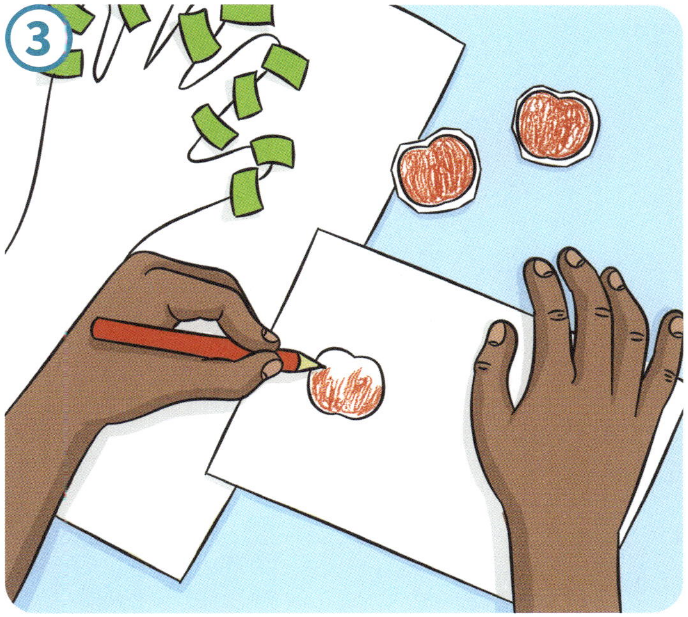

Review: The (apartment) is (new). The (tree) isn't (big). It's (small).

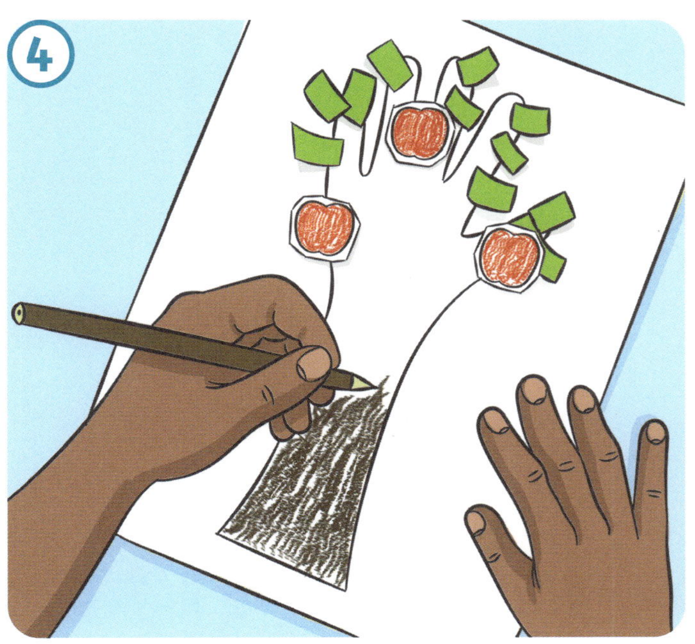

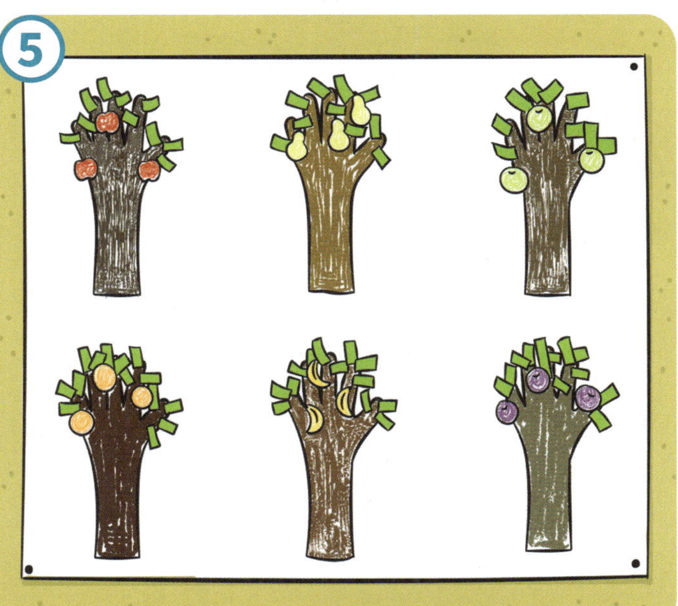

8 In the Kitchen

 Match.  Listen.  Point.

 Point.  Circle.  Draw.

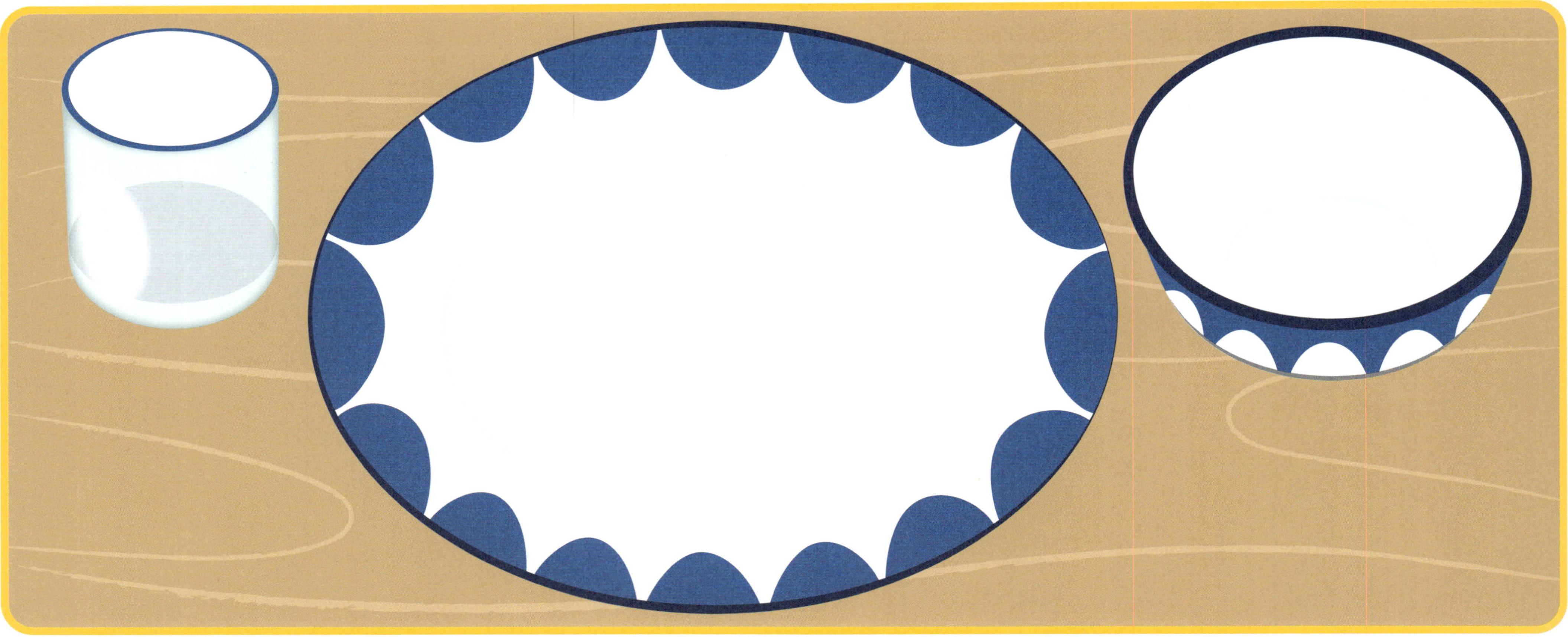

 Match. ◯ Circle.

 Think.  Match.  Draw.

 **Make.**  **Say.**

 Look.  Listen.  Circle.

 Look.  Match.  Check.

 Look.  Match.  Say.

 Look.  Circle.  Count.

Unit 9 Story Presentation

Think. Draw.

 Make.  Say.

O o

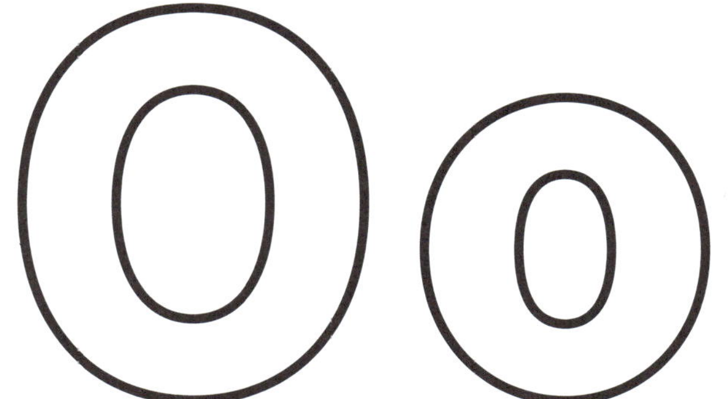

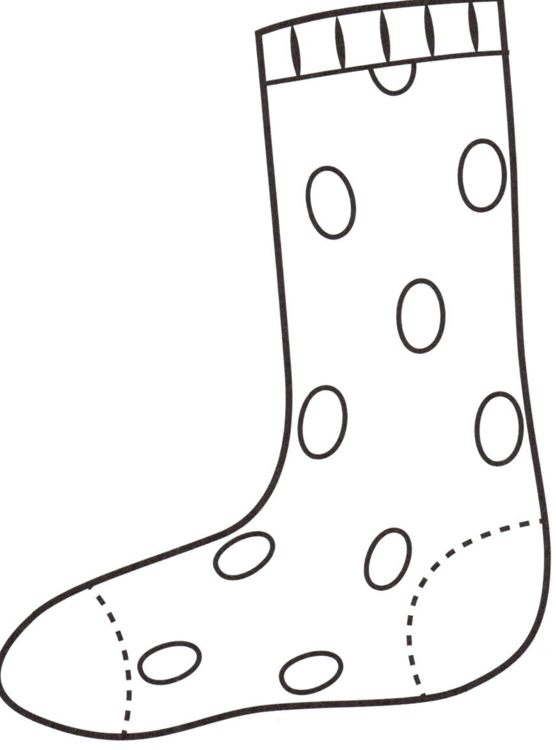

Uu

  Point.  Circle.  Say.

l   u   t

Point. Color. Say.

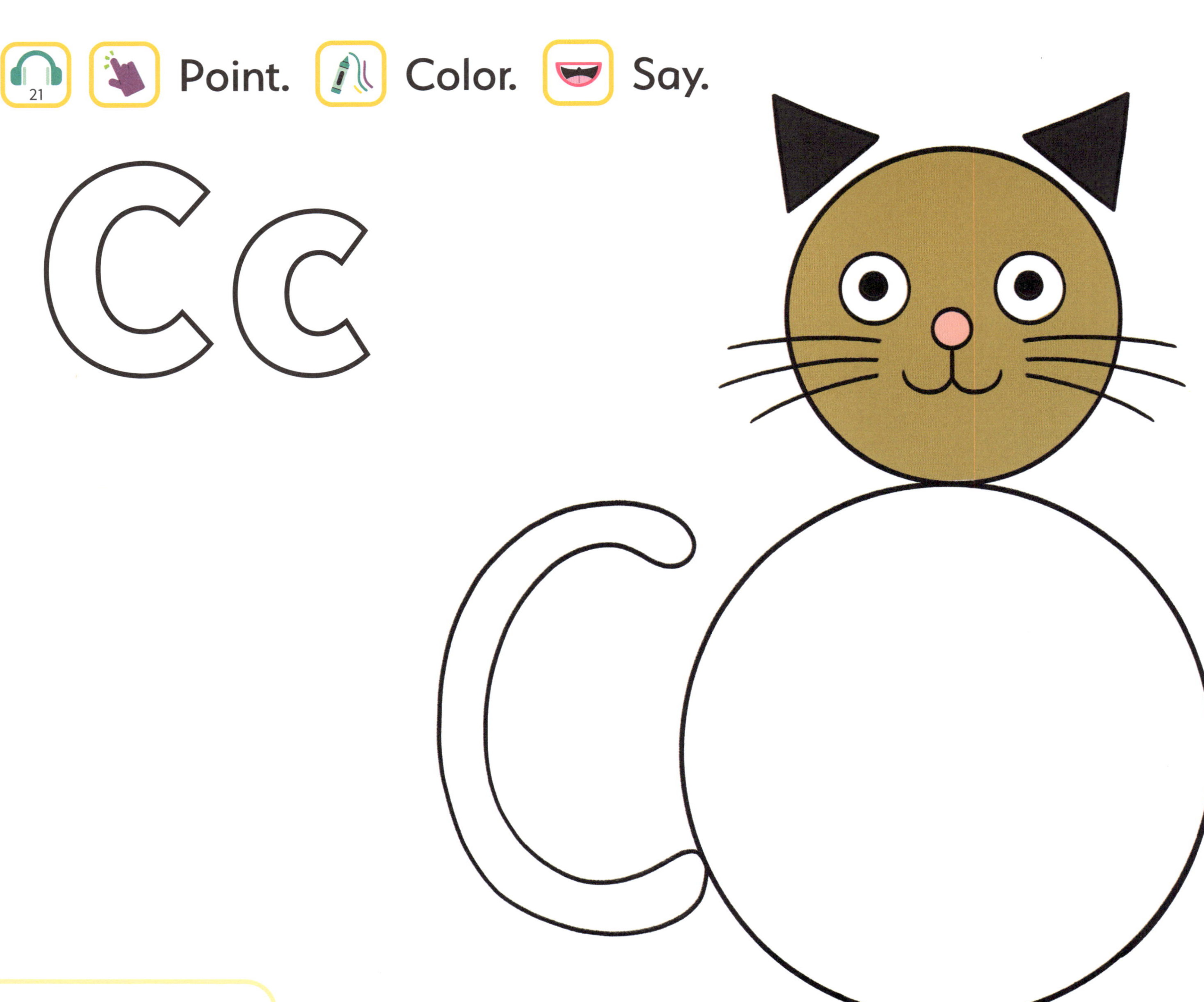

Rr

Ee

  Point.  Color.  Say.

Bb

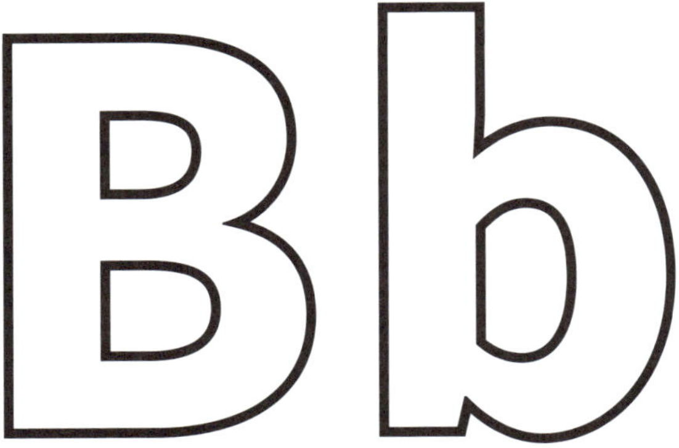

Ff

Circle.
Count.

 Count.  Color.  Say.

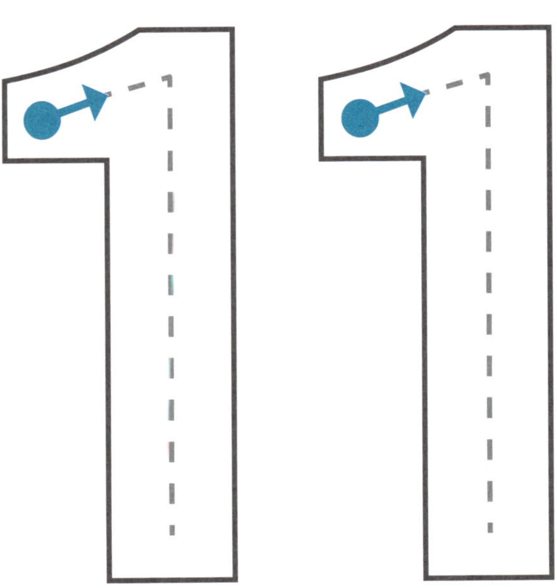

12

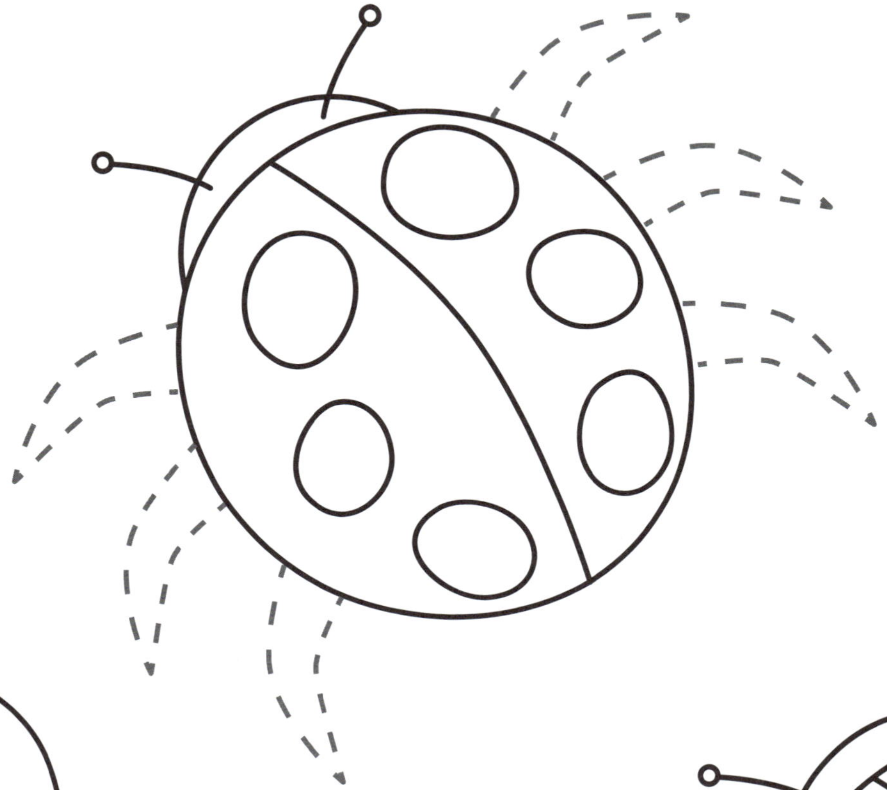

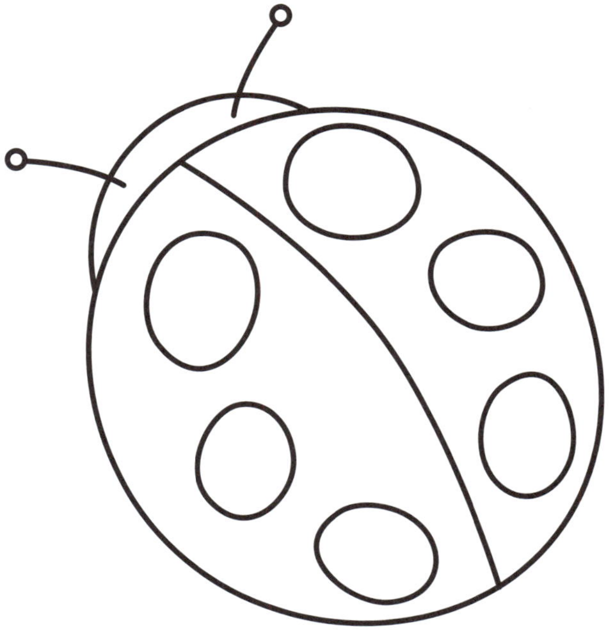

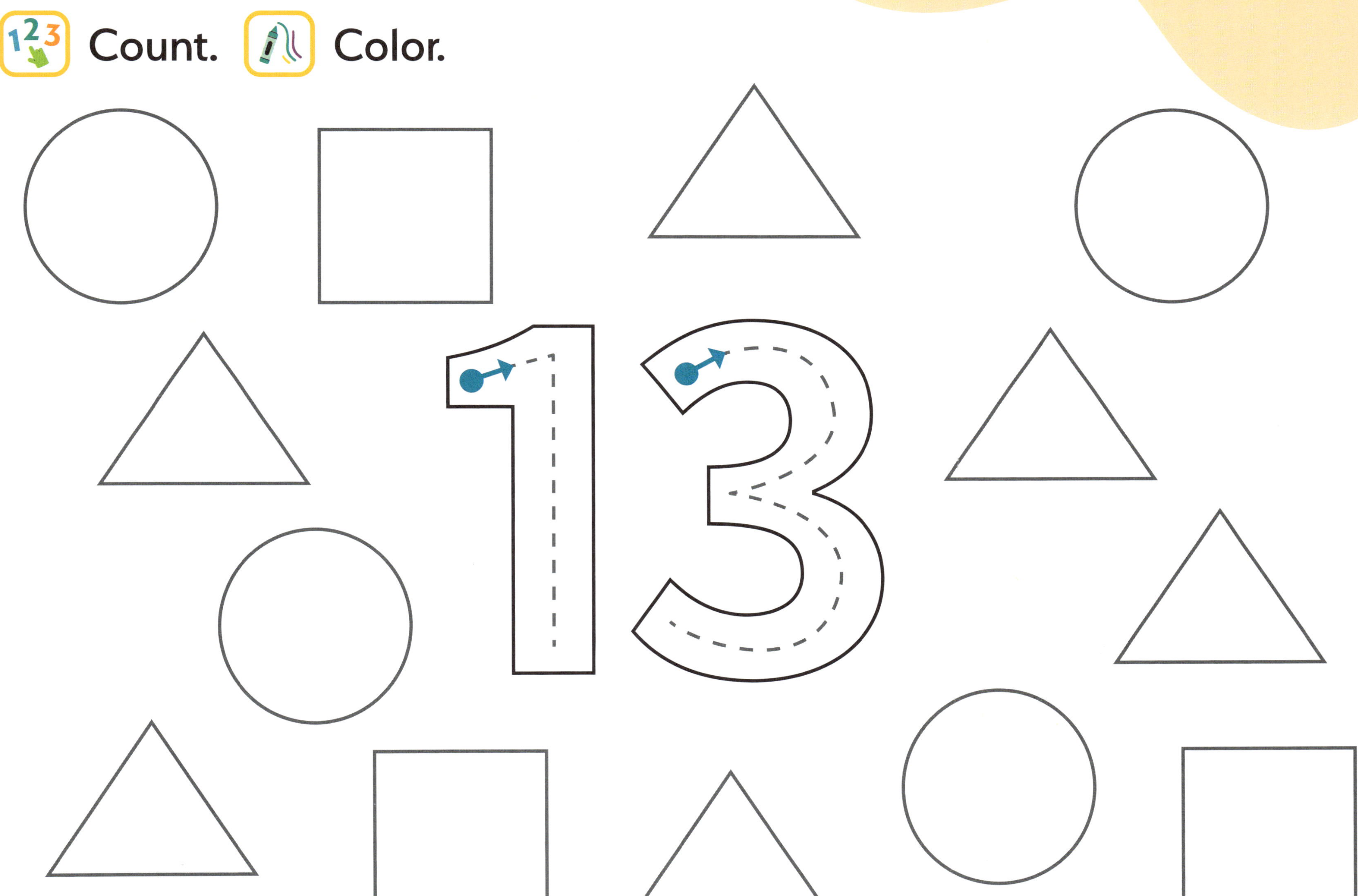

123 Count. Circle.
15

 Count.  Color.  Trace.

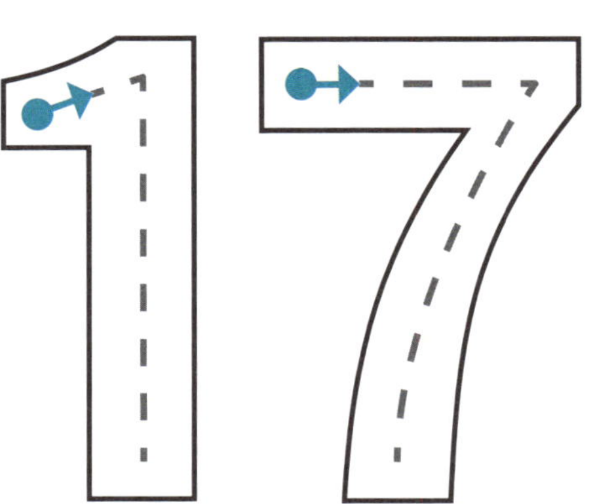

 Count.  Circle.  Trace.

16 17 18 19

20